hamlyn

ice creams

Notes

1 If using an ice cream maker, always follow the manufacturer's instructions.

2 The American Egg Board advises that eggs should not be consumed raw. This book contains some dishes made with raw or lightly cooked eggs. It is prudent for more vulnerable people, such as pregnant and nursing mothers, invalids, the elderly, babies and young children, to avoid uncooked or lightly cooked dishes made with eggs.

3 This book includes dishes made with nuts and nut derivatives. It is advisable for those with known allergic reactions to nuts and nut derivatives and those who may potentially be vulnerable to these allergies, such as pregnant and nursing mothers, invalids, the elderly, babies and children, to avoid dishes made with nuts and nut oils. It is also prudent to check the labels of pre-prepared ingredients for the possible inclusion of nut derivatives.

First published in 2001 by Hamlyn an imprint of Octopus Publishing Group Limited 2–4 Heron Quays, London, E14 4JP

Copyright © 2001 Octopus Publishing Group Limited

Distributed in the United States and Canada by Sterling Publishing Co., Inc. 387 Park Avenue South, New York, NY 10016-8810

ISBN 0 600 60591 4

Printed and bound in China

10 9 8 7 6 5 4 3 2 1

Photographer: Stephen Conroy
Food Stylist: David Morgan

Contents

introduction

Ices and ice creams are a universal favorite, appealing to people of all ages all over the world——in cold countries as well as hot ones, and as popular in Russia as in the tropics. Such is their appeal that they have been made out of almost every possible ingredient; ice creams made from tomatoes and asparagus were popular among the sophisticated between the two World Wars, and purple yam ice cream can be bought in the Philippines today.

Ice and Ice Creams in History

Chilled foods and wines are as old as civilization, for the histories of ice for storage and ices to eat are inextricably bound together. To have been in the happy position of being able to serve chilled food and ice to guests in hot weather must have been one of the world's first status symbols. The Mesopotamians, the Chinese, and the ancient Greeks and Romans all conserved snow and winter ice for use in the summer, and the first ice houses came into existence in about 2000 BC. In the 16th century, the Mughal emperors sent relays of horsemen to bring back ice and snow from the Hindu Kush for the fruit-flavored sherbets enjoyed by the rich and powerful in Delhi. In the 17th century, in Allahabad in Bengal, there was a four-acre site used for ice-making when the night-time temperatures were low enough and, at the same time, travelers in Persia seeing the ice houses in the great salt desert commented on the wonders of ice for preservation.

Cream ices originated in 17th-century Italy, still the home of some of the best ice cream in the world, and in May 1671 "one plate of Ice Cream" was served at Windsor Castle, the first recorded mention of a cream ice in England. In 1751, Mrs. Hannah Glasse included a recipe for raspberry ice cream in an edition of her book *The Art of Cookery Made Plain and Easy*; also in Frederic Nutt's *Complete Confectioner*, published in 1789, there were no less than 31 ice creams, including a selection of fruit flavors and chocolate, coffee, and pistachio—in fact, very much a selection that would be popular today. During the 18th century, water ices were preferred in France, Italy, and other parts of continental Europe, while the British and the Americans opted for cream ices.

Ice houses were slow to gain acceptance in Britain, but after the restoration of Charles II, who had an ice house built in St. James's Park, they became popular and by the middle of the 18th century, every country estate of any consequence, with its own lake, had an ice house. They were generally built of brick or stone and shaped like a well, with sloping sides about 12–15 feet deep, and with a soakaway at the bottom, and topped by a domed roof. They were insulated by layers of earth, surrounded by trees, and approached through a long tunnel, closed off by a series of doors. A vent in the roof helped to ensure dryness, for a damp atmosphere encouraged the ice to melt. The ice was cut from the lake, and carried or slid to the ice house and layered with straw for insulation.

During the 19th century, top-quality ice was exported from New England to Britain and the Caribbean (the most famous company was the Wenham Lake Ice Co. of Massachusetts), and Norway also supplied the UK, particularly ports in the north. Shipping ice was a hazardous business, for one-fifth of the cargo could melt on the voyage from the USA to Britain.

Ice creams have always been popular in the USA. George Washington's household goods included a "cream machine for making ice," while Dolley Madison, society hostess and wife of James Madison, the 4th president of the United States, served an ice cream topped with strawberries at their second inaugural ball. Captain Marryat,

author of *The Children of the New Forest*, who traveled extensively in the United States in 1837, recorded with surprise that "ice creams are universal and very cheap." In the early days, ice cream making required considerable strength and stamina on the part of the cook, for the lengthy hand beating required to make the ice cream mixture smooth as it froze. However, in the 1840s, Nancy Johnson, an American, invented the hand-cranked freezer, but sadly, she failed to patent her invention.

Two more American innovations came next. In 1874 the first ice cream soda (made of milk, flavored syrup, and a scoop of ice cream) made its appearance at the semicentennial of the Franklin Institute in Philadelphia; then, in 1881, an ice cream parlor in Two Rivers, Michigan, served the first ice cream sundae, with a topping of chocolate syrup. This new delicacy is said to have earned its name because initially it was for sale only as a Sunday treat.

Cones appeared independently on both sides of the Atlantic around the turn of the 20th century. Mrs. Agnes Marshall, proprietor of Marshall's School of Cookery in London, W1, and the author of several best-selling cookbooks, was particularly interested in ice cream. In *Fancy Ices*, published in 1894, there are recipes, with illustrations, for cones, which were filled with ices, piled on a serving dish, and served as a dinner party dessert, to be eaten with a spoon and fork. American cones were first seen at the St. Louis World's Fair in 1904, a fortuitous improvisation when the supply of ice cream dishes ran out.

The first domestic refrigerators appeared just before World War I, but in Britain, they remained out of most people's reach until the 1950s. In 1939 in Britain, only one house in 50 boasted a refrigerator; instead, they had ice boxes, wooden containers lined with zinc and usually insulated with felt, which had a compartment for blocks of ice. The ice was sold from door-to-door by itinerant salesmen with horse-drawn carts. The arrival of the domestic freezer in the 1960s made ice cream making comparatively easy, while recent developments in the form of sophisticated electric home ice cream makers have made it simplicity itself.

Making Ices

Ices have the great advantage for the busy hostess in that they must be made in advance and that, on the whole, they don't require very much of the cook's time, merely a lengthy wait while the mixture freezes. There are several different types of ices. Sorbets, sherbets, and granitas are all water-based ices, and are generally light and refreshing. Cream ices should be smooth, rich, and sumptuous, and frozen yogurt should have a sharp, fresh taste.

When making ices, it helps to know a little about the freezing process. Without any additions, a fruit purée, the basis of many ices, would freeze to the solid consistency of a popsicle, but when other ingredients, such as sugar, cream, gelatin, eggs, alcohol, and air, are added to the purée they prevent it from freezing quite so hard. In general, the higher the ratio of cream to the basic flavoring, the less beating is necessary. This means that if an ice contains a high proportion of water (a sherbet made with fruit juice, for example), then ice crystals will form easily and, for a smooth finish, the ice will need a considerable amount of beating and stirring. The quantity of sugar in a recipe is vital to ice creams and other frozen desserts. Too much sugar and the ice won't freeze properly; not enough and it will be hard to scoop.

Alcohol also retards freezing. Ices with a little alcohol are soft to scoop, but ices with too much may not freeze hard enough. Instead of risking a slushy finish, you can drizzle a little more liqueur or spirit over the ice at the table.

Varied textures can make ice creams more interesting. Rocky Road Ice Cream (see page 24) includes pieces of chocolate, marshmallows, and raisins. It is similar to the Russian *plombir*, a rich ice cream with ground almonds, raisins, and candied fruit—a sort of tutti-frutti. Plain ice cream flavored with toasted breadcrumbs, giving it a nutty flavor, was an old-English favorite, while large pieces of crushed meringue give vanilla ice cream an unusual finish.

Granitas These are usually made with fruit juice or coffee, sugar, and, sometimes, alcohol, and served ice cold in tall glasses, sometimes layered with cream, to be eaten with a spoon. Unlike sherbets and ice creams, they have a grainy texture. Granitas should not be made in an ice cream maker.

Sorbets, Sherbets, and Water Ices
Sorbets and water ices generally consist of a sugar syrup and fresh fruit, alcohol or other ingredient. Sherbets are very similar, but with the addition of beaten egg whites, used to lighten the mixture and give a smoother texture. These desserts are often served in sundae glasses or tall glasses like granitas.

Cream Ices These contain fats, usually in the form of cream and/or egg custard. Some cream ices are frozen to the correct consistency without further beatings, but although custard-based ice creams may include whipped cream, the custard base does not have sufficient air to prevent ice crystals from forming, so these ices must be beaten during freezing to get rid of any graininess which would otherwise spoil the texture of the finished dish. This only applies if you are making the ice cream by hand; if an ice cream maker is being used, the machine will do the beating while it is churning and freezing.

Sugar Boiling

Sugar syrups are the basis of many frozen desserts. The most accurate way to identify which of the different stages the syrup has reached during cooking is to use a sugar thermometer. Listed below are the temperatures for the different stages of sugar boiling that have been used in this book, together with quick, alternative tests which are easy to use if you do not have a sugar thermometer.

Thread Stage (225°F) Using a small spoon, remove a little of the syrup and let it fall from the spoon onto a dish. The syrup should form a fine thin thread.

Soft Ball (235–245°F) Using a small spoon, drop a small amount of the syrup into ice water. Mold the sticky syrup into a soft ball with the fingers. Remove the ball from the water. It should immediately lose its shape.

Hard Ball (248–266°F) Using a small spoon, drop a little syrup into ice water, then mold into a ball with your fingers. Remove the ball from the water. It should feel resistant to the fingers and still quite sticky.

Caramel (320–350°F) Using a small spoon, remove a little of the syrup and pour it onto a white saucer. The syrup should be a light golden brown color. Do not let it reach the final stage of dark caramel, when it loses its sweetness.

Ice Cream Dishes

A sorbet, sherbet, or ice cream can be served on its own, with a simple decoration (see page 11), or used as the base for a more complicated dish. Listed below are some famous composite ice cream dishes.

Baked Alaska A sponge cake topped with ice cream, surrounded by meringue, and baked for 3–4 minutes at high heat to cook the meringue. The meringue insulates the ice cream from the heat, so it is essential that there are no gaps in the meringue covering.

Banana Split A banana split lengthwise, with vanilla ice cream along its length, and drizzled with hot fudge sauce and topped with whipped cream, chopped nuts, and a Maraschino cherry.

Ice Cream Bombe Layers of ice cream are frozen, one at a time, in a spherical mold to create a pretty dinner party dessert.

Ice Cream Charlotte A charlotte mold is lined with lady fingers and filled with ice cream. It is often lavishly decorated with whipped cream.

Peach Melba A concoction of poached peaches with vanilla ice cream, topped with raspberry sauce. This dish was created by the great chef Escoffier for the Australian opera singer, Dame Nellie Melba, in the 1880s.

Decorating Ice Creams and Frozen Desserts

Ice creams and frozen desserts lend themselves to a huge range of decorations. Recipes for Butterscotch, Caramel, and Fudge sauces and for Walnut Tuiles are scattered throughout the book. Caramelized fruit goes well with any flavor ice cream that the fruit complements. For instance serve **Caramelized Cherries** with Cherry Chocolate Ice Cream (see page 19).

To make the Caramelized Cherries, pour ½ cup of water into a heavy saucepan and add ¾ cup of superfine sugar. Heat gently until the sugar has dissolved. Increase the heat and cook rapidly until the syrup begins to caramelize and is golden brown. The temperature will register 320–350°F on a sugar thermometer—caramel stage (see page 10), then remove from the heat. Dip the cherries into the caramel and place on a sheet of lightly oiled foil and let cool. Dip a fork into the caramel, then shake it quickly over the cherries to create a nest.

Citrus fruit ices look good with slices or twists of orange, lemon, or lime, or a **fruit syrup**.

To make the Fruit Syrup, pour 2 tablespoons of water into a heavy saucepan and add 2 tablespoons of honey and ⅓ cup of fruit. Heat until boiling, then pour through a wire mesh strainer. Discard the fruit and pour the syrup over the ice cream.

Candied Citrus Peel works very well with sorbets, fruit sherbets, or ice creams.

To make Candied Citrus Peel, pour ¼ cup of water into a heavy saucepan and add ½ cup of superfine sugar. Add finely chopped peel and heat gently until the sugar has dissolved and turned into a light syrup. Remove from the heat, drain the peel, and coat with a little superfine sugar.

Herbs, especially mint, lemon balm, and borage, and sprigs of red, white, or black currants, look good with many ices, as do **frosted leaves, edible flowers, and little fruits**, such as whole grapes or red currant sprigs. These are easy to prepare.

To make the Frosted Fruit or Flower, coat the chosen fruit or edible flower in lightly beaten egg white, then sprinkle superfine sugar over to cover. Set aside to dry on a wire rack or wax paper. Drying takes about 2 hours.

Chocolate shavings or grated chocolate go well with chocolate, coffee, and vanilla ice creams, while whipped cream adds a luscious finishing touch to most creamy ices. Nuts are another good topping, while crisp cookies, such as fan wafers, cat's tongue cookies, and amaretti, make a crunchy contrast to the smoothness of ice cream. **Pralines** are a perfect accompaniment to ices such as Honeyed Banana Ice Cream with Nuts (see page 40).

To make the Pralines, pour ¼ cup of water into a heavy saucepan and add ¾ cup of superfine sugar and 2 tablespoons of corn syrup. Simmer gently until the sugar has dissolved to make a caramel syrup. Place 1¼ cups of toasted almonds on a lightly oiled piece of foil and pour the syrup over. Let set for 1 hour. Once set break up into irregular pieces and serve with the ice cream.

A hot sauce, such as fudge or chocolate, makes another good contrast with the coldness of ice cream and can help soften an ice which has set too hard or has too grainy a texture. It is worth buying an ice cream scoop rather than serving ices with a spoon—the finished shape looks more attractive and professional.

Storing Ices

To keep them in the freezer, pack ices in rigid plastic boxes with tight-fitting lids, and transfer them to the refrigerator about 30 minutes before you want to serve them. The longer an ice has been stored, the more softening time it will need. Ice creams can be stored in the freezer for about 3 months, and sorbets and sherbets for 1–2 months. Granitas can't be stored in the freezer, as they will turn into a solid mass.

strawberry ice cream

1 lb. strawberries, hulled

¼ cup fresh orange juice

a scant cup superfine sugar

2 cups whipping cream

wild strawberries and strawberry syrup (see page 11), for decoration

1 Finely mash the strawberries and mix with the orange juice to form a smooth purée. Stir in the sugar.

2 Place the strawberry purée in an ice cream maker and pour in the cream. Churn and freeze following the manufacturer's instructions.

3 Transfer to a low, rectangular container and place in the freezer until needed. Serve either in scoops or slices and decorate with wild strawberries and strawberry syrup.

Serves 6
Preparation time: **15 minutes, plus freezing**

blackberry ice cream

1 lb. blackberries

2 tablespoons superfine sugar

½ cup water

¼ cup granulated sugar

3 egg yolks

2 cups light cream

2 tablespoons confectioner's sugar, sifted

2 tablespoons rosewater

1 Put the blackberries into a saucepan with the superfine sugar and simmer for 10 minutes or until tender. Press through a wire mesh strainer and let cool.

2 Put the water and granulated sugar in a pan and heat gently, stirring, until the sugar has dissolved. Increase the heat and boil steadily until the syrup reaches a temperature of 225°F on a sugar thermometer—thread stage (see page 10).

3 Place the eggs into a heatproof bowl and whisk until frothy. Place over simmering water and gradually whisk in the hot sugar syrup. Whisk steadily until creamy. Take off the heat and continue whisking until cool.

4 Mix the cream with the fruit purée, confectioner's sugar, and rosewater, and fold into the egg mixture. Pour into an ice cream maker, and churn and freeze, following the manufacturer's instructions.

5 Serve immediately or transfer to a container and place in the freezer until needed. Scoop into chilled glasses and serve.

Serves 8
Preparation time: **10 minutes, plus cooling and freezing**
Cooking time: **about 20 minutes**

mango ice cream

½ **cup water**

½ **cup superfine sugar**

1 ripe mango, peeled, halved, and pitted

2 tablespoons lemon juice

⅔ **cup heavy or whipping cream**

crisp wafer cookies, to serve (optional)

1 Put the water and sugar into a heavy saucepan and heat gently, stirring, until the sugar has dissolved. Increase the heat and boil steadily until the syrup reaches a temperature of 225°F on a sugar thermometer—thread stage (see page 10). Remove from the heat and let cool.

2 Purée the mango flesh in a food processor or blender with the lemon juice. Then stir the purée into the syrup.

3 Place the mixture into an ice cream maker and add the cream. Churn and freeze following the manufacturer's instructions.

4 Scoop the ice cream into serving dishes and serve with crisp wafer cookies, if you like.

Serves 4–6
Preparation time: **20 minutes, plus cooling and freezing**
Cooking time: **about 8 minutes**

lemon and orange ice cream

grated zest and juice of 1 lemon

grated zest and juice of 1 orange

3 eggs, separated

a scant cup superfine sugar

¼ cup heavy or whipping cream

1 Strain the fruit juices into a pan and heat gently. Meanwhile whisk together the egg yolks, half of the sugar, and the lemon and orange zest in a heatproof bowl until thick and creamy. Place over simmering water and gradually whisk in the hot fruit juice. Whisk steadily until creamy. Take off the heat and continue whisking until cool.

2 Whip the egg whites until stiff, then whisk in the remaining sugar. Fold into the egg mixture with the cream.

3 Turn the mixture into an ice cream maker and churn and freeze following the manufacturer's instructions.

4 Scoop into chilled glasses or coupes and serve.

Serves 6–8
Preparation time: **20 minutes, plus freezing**

peach ice cream

4 large, ripe peaches, total weight about 1½ lbs., peeled

½ cup confectioner's sugar

1 tablespoon lemon juice

2 tablespoons white wine

2 teaspoons granulated gelatin

4 egg yolks

1¼ cups heavy or whipping cream

waffle cones dipped in chocolate and pistachio nuts, for serving

1 Purée the peach flesh with the sugar in a food processor or blender. Mix together the lemon juice and wine in a small bowl and sprinkle over the gelatin.

2 Transfer the peach purée to a large heatproof bowl. Beat in the egg yolks. Place the bowl over a pan of gently simmering water and stir until the mixture thickens.

3 Put the bowl of gelatin mixture into a shallow pan of hot water and leave until it dissolves. Stir the gelatin into the peach mixture and let cool.

4 Place the peach mixture in an ice cream maker and pour in the cream. Churn and freeze following the manufacturer's instructions.

5 Serve with waffle cones dipped in melted dark chocolate and crushed pistachio nuts, if desired.

Serves 6–8
Preparation time: **20 minutes, plus cooling and freezing**
Cooking time: **15 minutes**

candied ginger ice cream

½ cup water

6 tablespoons granulated sugar

3 egg yolks

1¼ cups heavy or whipping cream

⅔ cup candied ginger, finely chopped

1 Place the water and sugar in a saucepan and heat gently, stirring, until the sugar has dissolved. Increase the heat and boil steadily until the syrup reaches a temperature of 225°F on a sugar thermometer—thread stage (see page 10).

2 Place the eggs in a heatproof bowl and whip until frothy. Place over simmering water and gradually whip in the hot sugar syrup. Whip steadily until creamy, then take off the heat and continue whipping until cool.

3 Mix the candied ginger into the cream and then fold into the thick and creamy mixture.

4 Turn into an ice cream maker and churn and freeze following the manufacturer's instructions.

Serves 4–6
Preparation time: **20 minutes, plus cooling and freezing**
Cooking time: **10 minutes**

rum and raisin ice cream

2 tablespoons rum

½ cup raisins

6 tablespoons sugar

½ cup water

3 egg yolks

1 teaspoon vanilla extract

2 cups heavy or whipping cream

1 Put the rum into a small bowl, add the raisins, and let macerate for 4 hours.

2 Meanwhile, put the sugar and water into a small heavy saucepan and stir occasionally over low heat until the sugar has dissolved. Increase the heat and boil rapidly for 5 minutes.

3 Place the egg yolks and vanilla extract in a heatproof bowl and whip until frothy. Place over simmering water and gradually whip in the hot sugar syrup. Whisk steadily until creamy, then take off the heat and continue whipping until cool.

4 Place the mixture in an ice cream maker. Add the cream and churn and freeze following the manufacturer's instructions. Once frozen, fold in the macerated raisins.

Serves 6
Preparation time: **20 minutes, plus macerating, cooling, and freezing**
Cooking time: **10 minutes**

cherry chocolate ice cream

14 oz. can pitted black cherries in syrup

1 tablespoon cornstarch

¼ lb. double chocolate chip cookies (about 8 cookies)

2½ oz. milk chocolate, broken into pieces

7 oz. dark chocolate, broken into pieces

2 cups heavy or whipping cream

2 tablespoons confectioner's sugar

2 teaspoons vanilla extract

1 cup thick yogurt

Caramelized Cherries (see page 11), for decorating (optional)

1 Drain the cherries, reserving the syrup. Blend a little of the syrup with the cornstarch in a small saucepan. Stir in the remaining syrup and bring to boil, stirring until thickened. Cook gently for 1 minute. Remove the pan from the heat, stir in the cherries, and let cool.

2 Put the chocolate cookies into a plastic bag and tap them gently with a rolling pin to break into small pieces. Crumble the milk chocolate pieces.

3 Melt the dark chocolate with ⅓ cup of the cream in a heatproof bowl, set over a pan of simmering water. Stir gently until smooth, then let cool slightly.

4 Whip the remaining cream in a bowl with the confectioner's sugar, vanilla extract, and yogurt, until the cream just starts to hold its shape. Stir in half the dark chocolate mixture. Gently fold in the pieces of cookie and milk chocolate.

5 Place spoonfuls of the remaining chocolate mixture and the cherries in syrup, over the cream mixture. Using a large metal spoon, gently fold all the ingredients together until combined, but still with a slightly rippled effect. Turn into a freezer container and freeze for at least 4 hours.

6 Transfer the ice cream to the refrigerator about 30 minutes before serving. Spoon into glasses and decorate with the Caramelized Cherries, if you like.

Serves 6–8
Preparation time: **20 minutes, plus cooling and freezing**
Cooking time: **4–5 minutes**

cherry almond ice cream

⅔ cup milk

⅔ cup ground almonds

1 egg and 1 extra yolk

½ cup superfine sugar

2–3 drops almond extract

1 lb. red cherries, pitted,
or 1 lb jar of cherry compôte

¼ cup slivered almonds

⅔ cup heavy or whipping cream

1 Pour the milk into a small saucepan and stir in the ground almonds. Bring to boil, then set aside.

2 Put the egg and the extra yolk into a heatproof bowl with the sugar, and beat until pale and thick. Pour in the milk and almond mixture. Place the bowl over a pan of gently simmering water and stir until thick. Stir in the almond extract and let cool.

3 Put the cherries into a food processor or blender and process to a purée, then stir them into the custard.

4 Toss the slivered almonds in a heavy pan over low heat to toast them. Let cool.

5 Place the cherry mixture in an ice cream maker and pour in the cream. Churn and freeze following the manufacturer's instructions. Once frozen, mix in the toasted almonds.

6 Serve the ice cream in individual glasses, cups, or bowls.

Serves 6
Preparation time: **20 minutes, plus cooling and freezing**
Cooking time: **20 minutes**

old-fashioned vanilla ice cream

1¼ cups light cream

1 vanilla bean

4 egg yolks

⅓ cup superfine sugar

1¼ cups heavy or whipping cream

red currants coated in confectioner's sugar, for decoration (optional)

Hot Caramel Sauce, for serving (see below)

1 Put the light cream and vanilla bean into a heavy saucepan, set over low heat, and bring to just below boiling point. Remove from heat and leave to infuse.

2 Meanwhile, put the egg yolks and sugar into a heatproof bowl and set over a pan of gently simmering water. Stir with a wooden spoon until thick and creamy, then gradually stir in the scalded light cream, discarding the vanilla bean. Continue stirring for about 15 minutes until the custard is thick enough to coat the back of the spoon. Remove the bowl from the heat and let cool.

3 Place the vanilla mixture in an ice cream maker and pour in the cream. Churn and freeze following the manufacturer's instructions.

4 Serve immediately or transfer to a container and place in the freezer until needed. Decorate with red currants coated in confectioner's sugar, if you like. Serve with Hot Caramel Sauce.

Serves 6
Preparation time: **10 minutes, plus cooling and freezing**
Cooking time: **25 minutes**

hot caramel sauce

1 cup water

½ cup superfine sugar

juice of ½ lemon

1 Pour ⅔ cup of the water into a heavy saucepan and add the sugar. Heat gently until the sugar has dissolved. Increase the heat and cook rapidly until the syrup begins to caramelize and is golden brown. The temperature will register 350°F on a sugar thermometer —caramel stage (see page 10).

2 Remove the pan from heat and gradually stir in the remaining water with the lemon juice. Let cool, then gently reheat the sauce before serving.

Makes 1¼ cups
Preparation time: **10 minutes**
Cooking time: **20 minutes**

rocky road ice cream

1 quart Double Chocolate Chip Ice Cream (see page 34)

1 cup white chocolate chips

1⅓ cups mini marshmallows

¼ cup raisins

for serving:

Hot Fudge Sauce (see page 30) or chocolate shavings

Plain ice creams can be enhanced using different ingredients, such as raisins, marshmallows, and chocolate chips, as in this classic variation on chocolate ice cream.

1 Transfer the ice cream to the refrigerator for 30–60 minutes to let it soften slightly.

2 Mix together the white chocolate chips, marshmallows, and raisins.

3 Turn the ice cream into a bowl and break it up with a spoon. Add the remaining ingredients to the bowl and mix until dispersed throughout the ice cream. Transfer to a freezer container, cover, and place in the freezer for several hours or overnight.

4 Serve spooned into glasses with hot fudge sauce or chocolate shavings.

Serves 6
Preparation time: **10 minutes, plus softening and freezing**

coconut ice cream

1½ cups milk

1½ cups dried coconut

1½ cups light cream

2 eggs

2 egg yolks

½ cup sugar

¼ teaspoon salt

1 Put the milk, coconut, and cream into a heavy pan and heat slowly until mixture just starts to simmer—about 15–20 minutes. Push the mixture through a fine wire mesh strainer, pressing out as much of the coconut liquid as possible. Discard the coconut from the strainer.

2 Put the eggs and egg yolks, sugar, and salt into a heatproof bowl and beat until thick and creamy. Place the bowl over a pan of simmering water, stir in some of the coconut cream mixture, then add the remainder and cook until the mixture is thick enough to coat the back of a spoon.

3 Leave to cool, then pour into an ice cream maker. Freeze following the manufacturer's instructions.

Makes about 1 quart
Preparation time: **15 minutes,**
    plus freezing
Cooking time: **15–20 minutes**

greengage plum ice cream

1 lb. greengage plums

1 tablespoon lemon juice

6 tablespoons soft brown sugar

1 whole egg, separated, and
1 extra yolk

2½ cups heavy or whipping cream

waffle cookies, for serving (optional)

1 Put the greengage plums in a saucepan with the lemon juice, cover, and simmer gently until they are very soft. Press the plum mixture through a wire mesh strainer into a heatproof bowl.

2 Stir the sugar into the plum pulp, then stir in the egg yolks. Place the bowl over a pan of gently simmering water and stir until the mixture thickens. Remove from the heat and set aside to cool, then chill in the refrigerator for 1 hour.

3 Put the plum mixture in an ice cream maker and pour in the cream. Churn and freeze following the manufacturer's instructions until half frozen.

4 Lightly whisk the egg white until it forms soft peaks and add to the half-frozen mixture. Continue to churn and freeze until completely frozen.

5 Serve the ice cream with waffle cookies, if desired.

Serves 4
Preparation time: **20 minutes, plus cooling and freezing**
Cooking time: **20 minutes**

chocolate ice cream

1¼ cups heavy or whipping cream

2 tablespoons milk

½ cup confectioner's sugar, sifted

½ teaspoon vanilla extract

¼ lb. (about 1⅓ cups) dark chocolate, broken into pieces

2 tablespoons light cream

for serving:

Chocolate Sauce (see below)

pieces of dark chocolate (optional)

1 Put the heavy cream and milk into a bowl and whisk until peaks start to form. Stir in the confectioner's sugar and vanilla extract. Pour the mixture into a shallow freezer container and freeze for 30 minutes or until the ice cream begins to set around the edges.

2 Place the chocolate in a heatproof bowl with the light cream, set over a pan of gently simmering water, and stir gently with a wooden spoon until melted and smooth. Set aside to cool.

3 Remove the ice cream from the freezer and spoon into a bowl. Add the melted chocolate and quickly stir it through the ice cream with a fork. Return the ice cream to the freezer container, cover, and freeze until set.

4 Transfer the ice cream to the refrigerator 30 minutes before serving, to soften slightly. Serve with chocolate sauce and pieces of dark chocolate, if desired.

Tip:
If the mixture separates at step **2**, add 2 tablespoons of water, and stir well.

Serves 4
Preparation time: **20 minutes, plus cooling and freezing**
Cooking time: **10 minutes**

chocolate sauce

⅔ cup water

3 tablespoons superfine sugar

5 oz. (about 5 squares) dark chocolate

1 Gently heat all the ingredients in a saucepan, stirring, until melted. Serve the sauce immediately.

Makes about ⅔ cup
Cooking time: **5 minutes**

mint chocolate chip ice cream

2 egg whites

⅔ cup superfine sugar

13 oz. can evaporated milk, chilled

½ teaspoon peppermint extract

1 cup finely chopped dark chocolate

1 Lightly whisk the egg whites until they form soft peaks, then gradually whisk in the sugar. Place the evaporated milk in a bowl with the peppermint extract and whisk until thick, then fold into the meringue mixture with the chocolate.

2 Turn into an ice cream maker and churn and freeze following the manufacturer's instructions.

3 Serve immediately in chilled dishes or transfer to a container and place in the freezer until needed.

Serves 8
Preparation time: **20 minutes
    plus freezing**

hot fudge sauce

¼ cup dark chocolate, broken into small pieces

2 tablespoons corn syrup

½ cup superfine sugar

1 tablespoon cocoa

5 tablespoons hot water

2 tablespoons butter

1 tablespoon cold water

1 Put the chocolate in a heavy saucepan with the corn syrup, sugar, cocoa and hot water. Stir over a gentle heat until melted.

2 Increase the heat and cook rapidly, without stirring, until the soft ball stage is reached (see page 10). Remove from the heat and gently stir in the butter and cold water.

Makes about ⅔ cup
Preparation time: **5 minutes**
Cooking time: **about 10 minutes**

chocolate and mascarpone ice cream with coffee syrup

1¼ cups superfine sugar

1½ cups water

10 oz. (3⅓ cups) finely chopped dark chocolate

3 oz. (1 cup) chocolate chips

8 oz. (1 cup) mascarpone cheese

2 tablespoons lemon juice

1¼ cups whipping cream

¼ cup coffee liqueur

1 Put 2 tablespoons of the sugar into a heavy saucepan with ⅔ cup of the water. Heat gently until the sugar dissolves, then bring to a boil and boil rapidly for 3 minutes. Transfer the syrup to a bowl, stir in the chopped chocolate, and let it melt. (If the syrup cools before the chocolate has melted, heat it briefly in the microwave.)

2 Reserve ⅓ cup of the chocolate chips. Finely chop the remainder. Beat the mascarpone in a bowl until softened. Stir in the lemon juice and the melted chocolate mixture.

3 Place the mascarpone and chocolate mixture in an ice cream maker and then pour in the cream. Churn and freeze following the manufacturer's instructions. Once frozen fold in the chopped chocolate chips. Transfer the ice cream to a container and place in the freezer while making the coffee syrup.

4 To make the coffee syrup, heat the remaining sugar and the remaining water in a small heavy saucepan until the sugar dissolves. Bring to a boil and boil for 5 minutes until syrupy. Remove from the heat and stir in the coffee liqueur. Let it cool, then chill until ready to serve.

5 Transfer the ice cream to the refrigerator about 30 minutes before serving to soften slightly. Stir the reserved chocolate chips into the syrup. Scoop the ice cream onto serving plates, spoon the coffee syrup over the ice cream, and serve immediately.

Serves 6
Preparation time: **30 minutes, plus cooling and freezing**
Cooking time: **10–15 minutes**

walnut tuiles

½ stick (¼ cup) butter

2 egg whites

a generous ⅓ cup superfine sugar

½ cup all-purpose flour, sifted

¼ cup coarsely chopped
walnut halves

a little confectioner's sugar, sifted

These French cookies can be served as an accompaniment to many of the ice cream recipes in this book. After baking, the cookies are pressed gently into shape, to resemble a curved ridge tile. They will set hard in about 1 minute, so it is advisable to cook and shape only three or four at a time. Because they need to be cooked on cool cookie sheets each time, it is a good idea to have three sheets in use.

1 Melt the butter gently over low heat and let cool. Whisk the egg whites in a bowl until frothy, then add the superfine sugar and beat for about 2–3 minutes until the mixture thickens. Gently fold in the sifted flour, melted butter, and chopped walnuts.

2 Lightly grease 3 cookie sheets. Drop 3 or 4 small spoonfuls of the mixture on to a sheet. Spread each cookie into a shallow round. Dust with a little sifted confectioner's sugar. Bake in a preheated oven at 400°F, for about 5 minutes, or until golden brown around the edges.

3 Carefully remove the cookies from the cookie sheets and place on a lightly greased rolling pin, pressing gently to make the tile shape. When set, place on a wire rack and let cool.

4 Cook the remaining cookies in the same way, using a cool cookie sheet for each batch.

Variation: Coarsely chopped hazelnuts or sliced almonds may be substituted for the walnuts.

Makes 20
Preparation time: **15 minutes**
Cooking time: **about 30 minutes**

double chocolate chip
ice cream

1¼ cups milk

6 tablespoons soft dark brown sugar

1 cup dark chocolate, broken into pieces

2 eggs, beaten

½ teaspoon vanilla extract

1¼ cups heavy or whipping cream

½ cup chocolate chips

1 Put the milk, sugar, and chocolate into a saucepan and heat gently until the chocolate has melted and the sugar dissolved. Pour the warm mixture onto the beaten eggs, stirring constantly.

2 Return the mixture to the pan and cook over low heat, stirring constantly, until the custard thickens very slightly. Strain the mixture into a bowl and add the vanilla extract. Let it cool.

3 Place the cooled custard in an ice cream maker and add the cream. Churn and freeze following the manufacturer's instructions. Once frozen stir in the chocolate chips.

4 Serve immediately in individual dishes. Alternatively, transfer the ice cream to a container and place in the freezer until needed.

Serves 4–6
Preparation time: **15 minutes, plus cooling and freezing**
Cooking time: **15 minutes**

chocolate maple ice cream

¼ cup raisins

¼ cup boiling water

2 egg yolks

¼ cup soft brown sugar

⅔ cup dark chocolate, broken into pieces

3 tablespoons maple syrup

1¼ cups heavy or whipping cream

cats' tongue cookies or wafer cookies, for serving

1 Place the raisins in a bowl and add the boiling water. Soak for 15 minutes, then drain and set aside.

2 In a large bowl, whisk the egg yolks and sugar until thick and pale. Combine the chocolate and maple syrup in a heatproof bowl and place over a pan of gently simmering water. Stir until the chocolate has melted. Let cool.

3 Place the chocolate and the egg mixture in an ice cream maker, then add the cream. Churn and freeze following the manufacturer's instructions.

4 Once frozen fold in the raisins. Transfer to a freezer container, cover, and freeze until firm.

5 Transfer the ice cream to the refrigerator 30 minutes before serving to soften slightly. Serve with cat's tongue cookies or wafer cookies, if you like.

Serves 4–6
Preparation time: **20 minutes, plus cooling and freezing**

butterscotch sauce

¼ cup butter

¼ cup turbinado or brown sugar

¼ cup corn syrup

⅔ cup milk

1 Put the butter, sugar, and corn syrup into a heavy saucepan. Heat gently until the sugar has dissolved. Increase the heat and cook rapidly until the syrup reaches a temperature of 235–245°F on a sugar thermometer—soft ball stage (see page 10).

2 Remove the pan from the heat and cool slightly, then slowly beat in the milk.

Makes 1¼ cups
Preparation time: **10 minutes**
Cooking time: **about 10 minutes**

pecan praline ice cream

1¼ cups light cream

1 egg and 2 extra yolks

½ cup superfine sugar

1¼ cups heavy or whipping cream

pecan praline:

½ cup superfine sugar

¾ cup pecan halves

1 Heat the light cream in a small pan to just below boiling point. Then remove from heat.

2 Put the egg, egg yolks, and sugar into a heatproof bowl and whisk together. Stir in the hot cream and place the bowl over a pan of simmering water. Stir constantly with a wooden spoon for about 20 minutes until the custard is thick enough to coat the back of the spoon. Strain into a clean bowl, cover, and leave to cool.

3 Meanwhile, make the praline. Place the sugar and pecans in a saucepan over medium heat until the sugar caramelizes. Do not stir. Pour the mixture onto a buttered baking sheet and leave until cold. When cold, either grate in a rotary grater or grind in a coffee grinder.

4 Place the egg custard in an ice cream maker and add the cream. Churn and freeze following the manufacturer's instructions. Once frozen mix in three-quarters of the praline.

5 To serve, scoop spoonfuls of the ice cream into a serving dish and sprinkle with the remaining praline.

Serves 6
Preparation time: **45 minutes, plus cooling and freezing**
Cooking time: **25–30 minutes**

apricot and amaretto ice cream

½ lb. (1¼–1½ cups) dried apricots

2 tablespoons Amaretto di Saronno

⅔ cup heavy or whipping cream

½ cup granulated sugar

⅔ cup water

2 egg whites

for serving:

Warm Toffee Sauce (see below)

amaretti cookies

1 Place the apricots in a saucepan and cover with cold water. Cover the pan and simmer gently for 15 minutes or until soft.

2 Drain the apricots, transfer to a food processor or blender, and process to a purée. Let cool, then transfer to a medium bowl, and stir in the liqueur. Whip the cream until it forms soft peaks, then gently fold it into the apricot purée.

3 Place the sugar and water in a heavy pan and heat gently until the sugar dissolves, stirring all the time, then boil, without stirring, until the syrup registers 235–245°F on a sugar thermometer—soft ball stage (see page 10).

4 Meanwhile, put the egg whites into a bowl and whisk until stiff. Slowly pour on the boiling syrup, beating the egg whites at high speed all the time, and continue to beat until cool.

5 Combine the apricot mixture and the egg white mixture, mixing well. Transfer the mixture to a freezer container, cover, and freeze until firm, without further beating. Serve with toffee sauce, if desired, and amaretti cookies.

Serves 4
Preparation time: **20 minutes, plus cooling and freezing**
Cooking time: **25 minutes**

warm toffee sauce

¾ stick (⅓ cup) butter

1 tablespoon corn syrup

6 tablespoons brown sugar

¼ cup evaporated milk

1 Place all the ingredients in a heavy saucepan and heat gently, stirring constantly with a wooden spoon, until the sugar has dissolved.

2 Bring to a boil, then remove the pan from the heat. Serve warm.

Serves 4–6
Preparation time: **5 minutes**
Cooking time: **10 minutes**

honeyed banana ice cream with nuts

1 lb. bananas, peeled

2 tablespoons lemon juice

3 tablespoons thick honey

⅔ cup plain yogurt

½ cup chopped nuts

⅔ cup heavy or whipping cream

2 egg whites

pralines (see page 11), for serving (optional)

1 Put the bananas into a bowl with the lemon juice and mash until smooth. Stir in the honey, followed by the yogurt and nuts, and beat well.

2 Place the banana mixture and the cream in an ice cream maker. Churn and freeze following the manufacturer's instructions until half frozen.

3 Lightly whisk the egg whites until they form soft peaks. Add to the ice cream maker and continue to churn and freeze until completely frozen. Serve with pralines, if you like.

Serves 4–6
Preparation time: **15 minutes, plus freezing**

chocolate truffle and coffee
ice cream

1⅓ **cups finely chopped dark chocolate**

2 **tablespoons light cream**

2 **tablespoons rum**

2 **tablespoons instant coffee**

2 **tablespoons boiling water**

2 **egg whites**

⅔ **cup superfine sugar**

1¼ **cups heavy or whipping cream**

Walnut Tuiles (see page 32), for serving (optional)

1 To make the truffle mixture, place the chocolate, cream, and rum in a heatproof bowl over a pan of simmering water and leave until the chocolate has melted. Mix well, then set aside to cool.

2 To make the ice cream, dissolve the coffee in the boiling water and let cool. Whisk the egg whites until stiff, then whisk in the sugar. Whip the cream with the coffee until it forms soft peaks. Fold the coffee cream into the meringue mixture.

3 When the chocolate truffle mixture begins to thicken, stir it until it is smooth and soft, then fold it into the ice cream mixture very lightly to create a marbled effect. Turn into a freezer container, cover, and freeze until firm.

4 Transfer the ice cream to the refrigerator 30 minutes before serving, to soften slightly. Scoop into chilled sundae glasses and serve with walnut tuiles, if you like.

Serves 8
Preparation time: **15 minutes, plus cooling and freezing**
Cooking time: **10 minutes**

cinnamon pear ice cream

1 lb. ripe pears, peeled, cored, and chopped

2 tablespoons lemon juice

2 tablespoons corn syrup

½ stick (¼ cup) butter

1 teaspoon ground cinnamon

1 egg and 1 extra egg yolk

⅔ cup heavy or whipping cream

mint leaves, for decoration

1 Place the pears in a saucepan with the lemon juice, corn syrup, butter, and cinnamon. Bring slowly to a boil, then simmer uncovered until the pears are soft. Purée the pears in a food processor or blender, then return the purée to the rinsed pan.

2 Put the egg and the extra yolk into a bowl and beat together. Stir the beaten eggs into the pear mixture, then place the pan over a very gentle heat and continue to stir until the mixture thickens. Set aside to cool.

3 Transfer the pear mixture to an ice cream maker and add the cream. Churn and freeze following the manufacturer's instructions. Serve in individual dishes and decorate with mint leaves.

Serves 4–6
Preparation time: **20 minutes, plus cooling and freezing**
Cooking time: **20 minutes**

peppermint ice cream

two 7-inch long pieces or 2 oz.
peppermint candy

4 egg yolks

⅓ cup superfine sugar

1 teaspoon cornstarch

1¼ cups milk

1¼ cups heavy or whipping cream

extra crushed peppermint candy,
for decoration (optional)

1 Put the peppermint candy into a plastic bag and beat with the end of a rolling pin until roughly crushed. Continue to beat until the candy is broken into small granules.

2 Beat the egg yolks in a bowl with the sugar, cornstarch, and a little of the milk until smooth. Bring the remaining milk to a boil in a heavy saucepan. Pour the milk over the egg yolk mixture, whisking well until combined. Return the mixture to the saucepan and cook very gently, stirring until it has thickened enough to coat the back of the spoon thinly.

3 Transfer the custard to a bowl, cover with a circle of wax paper to prevent a skin from forming, and let cool. Chill in the refrigerator until very cold.

4 Place the custard mixture in an ice cream maker and add the cream and candy granules. Churn and freeze following the manufacturer's instructions.

5 Serve immediately or transfer to a container and place in the freezer until needed. Scoop into glasses and sprinkle with extra crushed peppermint candy, if you like.

Serves 4
Preparation time: **20 minutes,
plus freezing**
Cooking time: **5 minutes**

lavender honey ice cream with roasted figs

6 tablespoons lavender honey

4 egg yolks

1 teaspoon cornstarch

1 tablespoon sugar

1¼ cups milk

1¼ cups heavy or whipping cream

lavender sprigs, for decoration (optional)

roasted figs:

4 large fresh figs

2 tablespoons honey

1 tablespoon fresh orange juice

If you can't get lavender-flavored honey, use another mild flower honey and add the flowers of eight lavender sprigs to the custard.

1 Put the honey, egg yolks, cornstarch, and sugar into a bowl and whisk lightly to combine. Bring the milk to a boil in a heavy saucepan. Pour the milk over the egg yolk mixture, whisking well until combined. Return the mixture to the saucepan and cook very gently, stirring constantly, until the custard has thickened enough to coat the back of the spoon thinly. Transfer to a bowl and cover with a round of wax paper to prevent a skin from forming. Let cool, then chill in the refrigerator until very cold.

2 Transfer the custard to an ice cream maker and add the cream. Churn and freeze following the manufacturer's instructions.

3 Meanwhile, to cook the figs, cut a cross in the top of each fig and place each one in a shallow ovenproof dish. Brush the figs with the honey and drizzle with the orange juice. Roast in a preheated oven at 425°F, for about 10 minutes or until lightly caramelized around the edges.

4 Serve the ice cream immediately or transfer to a container in the freezer until needed. Scoop into glasses and serve with the figs, spooning over any juices. Decorate with lavender sprigs, if you like.

Serves 4
Preparation time: **20 minutes, plus chilling and freezing**
Cooking time: **15 minutes**

summer berry sorbet

8 oz. frozen mixed summer berries

⅓ cup spiced berry cordial

2 tablespoons Kirsch or vodka

1 tablespoon fresh lime juice

For an elegant summer dessert, you can make three types of berry sorbet and serve them together.

1 Chill a shallow freezer container. Put the berries, cordial, Kirsch or vodka, and lime juice into a food processor or blender and process until smooth. Do not over-blend, as this will soften the mixture too much.

2 Turn the purée into the chilled container, cover, and freeze for at least 25 minutes.

3 Spoon the sorbet into bowls and serve.

Serves 2
Preparation time: **5 minutes, plus freezing**

roasted plum sorbet

1½ lbs. plums, cut in half and pitted

1⅓ cups superfine sugar

2½ cups water

1 cinnamon stick

strip of lemon zest

for decoration:

1 plum, cut into 4 slices

mint sprigs

1 Place the plums in a roasting pan and cook in a preheated oven at 400°F, for 45 minutes.

2 Put the sugar, water, cinnamon stick and lemon zest into a saucepan. Slowly dissolve the sugar over low heat and bring to boil. Cook over medium heat for 20 minutes until the mixture is syrupy.

3 Transfer the cooked plums to the sugar syrup and cook for a further 10 minutes. Remove the pan from the heat, and discard the lemon zest and cinnamon stick.

4 Purée the fruit mixture in a food processor or blender or press through a wire mesh strainer. Let cool.

5 Transfer the purée to an ice cream maker and freeze following the manufacturer's instructions.

6 Serve immediately or transfer to a container and place in the freezer until needed. Scoop into glasses and decorate with plum slices and mint sprigs.

Serves 4
Preparation time: **10 minutes, plus cooling and freezing**
Cooking time: **55 minutes**

tangerine sorbet

10 tangerines

a scant cup superfine sugar

6 tablespoons water

juice of 2 lemons

mint sprigs, for decoration

orange flavored liqueur,
for serving (optional)

This refreshing sorbet is the perfect dessert after a rich main course or as a cooling treat on a hot summer's afternoon.

1 Peel the tangerines. Cut the segments in half and discard the seeds. Purée the flesh in a food processor or blender, then press through a wire mesh strainer to extract as much juice as possible. Transfer the juice to a measuring cup or bowl.

2 Put the sugar and water into a heavy saucepan and heat until the sugar has dissolved. Bring to a boil and boil for 3 minutes or until syrupy.

3 Add the syrup to the tangerine juice with the lemon juice. You will need about 1 quart of liquid. Make it up with extra tangerine juice or fresh orange juice, if necessary.

4 Pour the mixture into an ice cream maker and freeze following the manufacturer's instructions.

5 Serve immediately or transfer to a container and place in the freezer until needed. Pile into glasses, decorate with mint sprigs, and drizzle with a little orange liqueur, if you like.

Serves 6
Preparation time: **10 minutes, plus freezing**
Cooking time: **5 minutes**

fresh pineapple sherbet

2 cups water

½ cup plus 2 tablespoons sugar

1 strip of lemon zest

1 fresh ripe pineapple, weighing about 2½ lbs.

2 teaspoons granulated gelatin

1 Put the water, sugar, and lemon zest into a heavy saucepan and heat gently until the sugar has dissolved. Bring to boil, then boil for 5 minutes until syrupy. Remove from heat, let cool, then remove and discard the lemon zest.

2 Meanwhile, cut the pineapple in half lengthwise and scoop out the flesh. Reserve the shells, wrap them closely in foil, and chill in the refrigerator until serving time. Purée the flesh in a food processor or blender, and then measure out 2 cups.

3 Pour ⅔ cup of the cooled syrup into a small bowl and sprinkle the gelatin over it. Stir to dissolve, then leave for 5 minutes. Stand the bowl in a pan of simmering water and heat gently until completely dissolved. Stir the dissolved gelatin mixture into the remaining syrup, then leave until completely cold.

4 Transfer the syrup and pineapple purée to an ice cream maker and freeze following the manufacturer's instructions.

5 Serve immediately or transfer to a container and place in the freezer until needed. Scoop into the chilled pineapple shells to serve.

Serves 4–6
Preparation time: **30 minutes, plus cooling and freezing**
Cooking time: **10 minutes**

apricot and orange sherbet

¾ **cup superfine sugar**

1¼ **cups water**

⅓ **cup fresh orange juice**

3 **tablespoons fresh lemon juice**

grated zest of 1 orange

1 **lb. ripe apricots, cut in half and pitted**

1 **egg white**

sugared mint strips, for decoration (optional)

1 Put the sugar, water, orange and lemon juices, and orange zest into a saucepan and bring to a boil, stirring until the sugar has dissolved. Increase the heat and boil rapidly for about 5 minutes until the syrup registers 225°F on a sugar thermometer—thread stage (see page 10). Add the apricots and simmer gently for about 2 minutes, until they have softened slightly. Let them cool in the syrup.

2 Pour the fruit and syrup into a food processor or blender and process to a smooth purée.

3 Transfer the mixture to an ice cream maker and freeze. Follow the manufacturer's instructions until half frozen. Whisk the egg white until it forms soft peaks and add to the half-frozen mixture. Churn and continue to freeze until completely frozen.

4 To serve, arrange scoops of sherbet in individual glasses and decorate with sugared mint strips, if you like.

Serves 6–8
Preparation time: **20 minutes, plus cooling and freezing**
Cooking time: **8 minutes**

fresh melon sherbet

1 cantaloupe, weighing 2 lbs.

½ cup confectioner's sugar

juice of 1 lime or 1 small lemon

1 egg white

Other flavorful melons, such as honeydew or watermelon, may be used for this sherbet. For a dinner party, make three sherbets using different types of melon: the different colored flesh and subtly different flavors make a very special dessert.

1 Cut the melon in half and scoop out and discard the seeds. Scoop out the melon flesh with a spoon and discard the shells.

2 Place the flesh in a food processor or blender with the confectioner's sugar and lime or lemon juice. Process to a purée, then pour into an ice cream maker and freeze. Follow the manufacturer's instructions, until the mixture is half frozen.

3 Lightly whisk the egg white until it forms soft peaks, then stir it into the half-frozen mixture. Churn and continue to freeze until completely frozen.

4 Serve immediately or transfer to a container and place in the freezer until needed. Scoop the sherbet into glass dishes to serve.

Serves 4–6
Preparation time: **15 minutes, plus freezing**

tangy lemon sherbet

2½ cups water

1 cup sugar

3 tablespoons water

1 tablespoon granulated gelatin

zest of 2 lemons

1¼ cups fresh lemon juice

2 egg whites

Candied Lemon Peel (see page 11), for serving (optional)

1 Put the 2½ cups water and sugar into a small pan and heat gently until the sugar dissolves. Bring to a boil and boil steadily for 10 minutes. Let cool.

2 Put the 3 tablespoons water in a small bowl and sprinkle the gelatin over it. Set the bowl over a pan of simmering water and leave until the gelatin goes spongy. Whisk the gelatin mixture into the syrup along with the lemon zest and juice.

3 Pour the lemon mixture into an ice cream maker. Churn and freeze, following the manufacturer's instructions, until half frozen.

4 Lightly whisk the egg whites until they form soft peaks. Add to the half-frozen mixture and continue to churn and freeze until completely frozen.

5 Serve immediately or transfer to a container and place in the freezer until needed. Decorate with candied lemon peel, if desired.

Makes 1 quart
Preparation time: **15 minutes, plus cooling and freezing**
Cooking time: **10–15 minutes**

pear sherbet

1 lb. ripe eating pears, peeled, cored, and sliced

2 tablespoons lemon juice

2 tablespoons honey

2 egg whites

1 Place the pears, lemon juice, and honey in a medium saucepan. Cover, and simmer until the fruit is soft.

2 Purée the pears in a food processor or blender and let cool. Spoon into an ice cream maker and churn until half-frozen, following the manufacturer's instructions.

3 Whisk the egg whites until they form soft peaks and add to the half-frozen mixture. Continue to churn and freeze until completely frozen.

Serves 4
Preparation time: **15 minutes, plus cooling and freezing**
Cooking time: **10 minutes**

blood orange granita

2 lbs. blood oranges

1 cup sugar

1 Using a sharp knife, cut off the tops and bottoms of the oranges, then cut away the pith and peel. Working over a bowl to catch the juice, cut the segments out of the oranges and squeeze any excess juice from them.

2 Strain the juice into a saucepan, add the sugar, and heat gently until it has completely dissolved.

3 Place the orange flesh in a food processor or blender, and process until smooth. Stir in the juice, then pour into ice cube trays and freeze until firm.

4 Chill the serving glasses briefly in the freezer before serving. To serve, remove the granita cubes from the freezer, put them in the food processor or blender and process for 30 seconds, then transfer the ice to the chilled glasses and serve immediately.

Serves 4
Preparation time: **10 minutes,**
   plus freezing
Cooling time: **5 minutes**

orange and passion fruit granita

2¼ cups fresh orange juice

2 passion fruit

4–6 teaspoons Grenadine

1 Pour the orange juice into a bowl. Cut the passion fruit in half and squeeze out the pulp. Stir into the juice and then pour into ice cube trays and freeze until firm.

2 To serve, first chill 4–6 tall glasses in the refrigerator for 15–20 minutes, then remove the granita cubes from the freezer, put them into a food processor or blender and process for 30 seconds.

3 Spoon the granita into the chilled glasses and top each portion with 1 teaspoon of Grenadine.

Serves 4–6
Preparation time: **10 minutes,**
   plus freezing

lemon honey granita

4 large or 6 medium lemons

about 4 tablespoons water

2 tablespoons honey

⅓ cup sugar

1 fresh bay leaf or 1 lemon balm sprig

2 cups plain yogurt or fromage frais

lemon balm sprigs, for decoration

1 Cut a slice from the base of each lemon so that it will stand upright without wobbling.

2 Slice the top off of each lemon and reserve. Carefully scoop out all the pulp and juice with a teaspoon; do this over a bowl, so that no juice is wasted. Discard any white pith, skin, and seeds from the flesh. Strain or blend the pulp and juice. You need ⅔ cup. If there is less than this, make it up with water. Cut out any excess pith from the lemon shells and from the reserved tops.

3 Put the measured water into a saucepan with the honey, sugar, and bay leaf or lemon balm. Stir over low heat until the sugar has dissolved, then let cool. Combine with the lemon purée and the yogurt or fromage frais. Do not remove the herb at this stage.

4 Pour into a shallow freezer container, cover, and place in the freezer until lightly frozen, then gently fork the mixture and remove the herb. Re-freeze the granita for a short time, until it is firm enough to spoon into the lemon shells. Replace the tops of the lemons and place the fruit in the freezer.

5 Transfer the granitas to the refrigerator about 20 minutes before serving. Serve decorated with lemon balm sprigs.

Variation: Use 4–6 oranges instead of lemons. Honey isn't as nice with oranges, so omit it and use just the sugar. Use a mixture of half orange purée and half yogurt or fromage frais.

Serves 4–6
Preparation time: **20 minutes, plus cooling and freezing**
Cooking time: **5 minutes**

coffee granita

¼ cup freshly ground strong coffee beans

⅔ cup superfine sugar

2 cups boiling water

whipped cream, for serving (optional)

1 Put the ground coffee and sugar into a cup and stir in the boiling water. Stir until the sugar has dissolved, then let cool.

2 Strain the coffee liquid into a freezer container, cover, and chill in the refrigerator for about 30 minutes. Transfer to the freezer and freeze for at least 2 hours or until completely solid.

3 Remove the granita from the container, then quickly chop it into big chunks with a large strong knife. Return it to the container and freeze until just hard. Serve straight from the freezer, with whipped cream if you like.

Serves 4
Preparation time: **10 minutes, plus cooling and freezing**

campari granita

½ cup superfine sugar

⅔ cup water

2 cups fresh orange juice

¾ cup Campari

1 Heat the sugar and water in a saucepan until the sugar has dissolved, then bring to a boil and boil for 3 minutes. Let cool.

2 Mix the syrup with the juice and Campari and pour into a shallow freezer container. Cover and freeze for about 2 hours or until a thick layer of ice crystals has formed around the edges.

3 Using a fork, break up the ice crystals, stirring them into the center of the container. Return the granita to the freezer for another 30 minutes or until more ice crystals have formed around the edges.

4 Repeat the forking and freezing until the mixture has the consistency of crushed ice. Freeze until ready to serve.

5 To serve, lightly stir the granita with a fork and pile it into tall glasses.

Serves 4
Preparation time: **15 minutes, plus freezing**
Cooking time: **5 minutes**

champagne water ice

1 cup sugar

1¼ cups water

1¼ cups Champagne

juice of 1 lemon and 1 orange

strawberries, for serving

1 Put the sugar and water into a heavy saucepan and heat until the sugar has dissolved.

2 Stir the Champagne and fruit juices into the sugar syrup, then pour into an ice cream maker. Churn and freeze following the manufacturer's instructions.

3 Serve immediately or transfer to a container in the freezer until needed. Serve with strawberries.

Serves 6
Preparation time: **15 minutes, plus cooling and freezing**
Cooking time: **5–10 minutes**

citrus and rum sherbet

1½ teaspoons granulated gelatin

½ cup cold water

½ cup superfine sugar

1 tablespoon fresh lime juice

¼ cup white rum

½ cup fresh orange juice

1½ teaspoons grated orange zest

fresh mint leaves, or fine strips of candied orange peel (see page 11), for decoration

1 Sprinkle the gelatin over 2 tablespoons of the water in a small heatproof bowl. Leave until spongy, then stand the bowl in a pan of simmering water. Heat gently, stirring, until the gelatin has dissolved, then remove the bowl from the heat.

2 Bring the sugar and the remaining water to a boil in a small, heavy saucepan and simmer for 1 minute. Stir in the dissolved gelatin. Add the lime juice, rum, orange juice, and zest and cook for 30 seconds over low heat. Remove from heat and let cool.

3 Strain the mixture into an ice cream maker. Churn and freeze following the manufacturer's instructions. Scoop the sherbet into glasses and serve decorated with mint or candied orange peel.

Serves 4
Preparation time: **15 minutes, plus cooling and freezing**
Cooking time: **5 minutes**

index